WORDS,
MEANINGS
AND PEOPLE

INTERNATIONAL SOCIETY FOR GENERAL SEMANTICS
SAN FRANCISCO

International Society for General Semantics
P.O. Box 2469
San Francisco, California 94126

ISBN 0-918970-31-8
LCCCN 82-084221

*This book is dedicated
to the memory of the late Professor Irving J. Lee
of Northwestern University.*

*"There are always in the world a few
inspired men whose acquaintance is beyond price."*
– Plato

Contents

THE IMPORTANCE OF ATTITUDE
IN PERSONAL RELATIONS

LIVING IN A NON-VERBAL WORLD

Foreword

What is so mysterious about using words and language to communicate? Why do we have so many communication problems? Isn't it simply a matter of choosing the right words with the right meanings for listeners to completely understand our messages? How about words that can be given more than one meaning? Should we try to eliminate all ambiguous words from our vocabularies? Do words contain meaning, as we are taught? Why do we jump to conclusions? How do we deal with the "closed mind"?

These are but a few of the questions dealt with in these brief articles on general semantics. The author also examines the fundamental building blocks we use to shape thoughts about ourselves and our world: our conscious and unconscious assumptions. He looks at the problems arising when we confuse *what* we observe with our inferences, our conclusions, or our judgments.

He includes articles on recognizing human limitations, the closed mind, and how to cope with the rigidities of the know-it-all attitude. He explores the role language can play in producing more flexible attitudes and helping us get along with others. In short, he demonstrates — aided by many examples — how to apply general semantics principles to improve thinking ability, communicate effectively and build more productive human relationships.

A long-time teacher and lecturer, the author is free to draw on a multitude of resources and experiences in discussing practical applications of general semantics. In addition to the four books he has written — *Why Do We Jump to Conclusions?*, *The Closed Mind, How to Lessen Misunderstandings,* and *Understanding and Being Understood* — he has prepared a number of tape recorded instructional programs on general semantics for schools, business and industry.

The pieces in this collection were first published as columns in the "San Diego Evening Tribune." Since they were written for the casual news reader who might see an occasional column, several important principles and key points are discussed more than once.

Such repeated emphases may be welcomed by readers, especially newcomers to general semantics who are eager to grasp the principles and applications quickly and put them to work in their own thinking and communication.

Russell Joyner
Executive Director
International Society
for General Semantics
Co-author of *How to Write Clearly*

WORDS, MEANINGS AND COMMUNICATION

1
Words, meanings and people

When Fred Kinne, editor of "The Evening Tribune," asked me to write these columns, he requested that I write some on general semantics. He had long been a student of semantics, English and good writing habits, and he knew of the values of general semantics in everyday life.

My interest in general semantics goes back many years. When I was a student in junior college in my home town of Virginia, Minn., I reviewed Stuart Chase's book, *The Tyranny of Words*. This was the first popularization of Alfred Korzybski's scholarly book *Science and Sanity*. In *Science and Sanity* Korzybski explained how language habits are inadequate in our common world today. Korzybski's book was published in 1933 and offered methods by which we could learn new language habits. Chase's book, published in 1938, introduced some of Korzybski's ideas to a mass audience, although some of these ideas were misrepresented.

It was not until 1941, when Dr. S.I. Hayakawa's *Language in Action* was published, that a national audience was familiar with some of the ideas of general semantics. Dr. Hayakawa's book was a Book-of-the-Month Club selection and has been used continually in English classes.

What is general semantics? My simple definition is that general semantics is the study of the relationship between language, thought and human behavior. The kind of language we use is related to the kind of thinking that we do.

Because the Chinese have a different structure in their language, the structure of their thinking is different. Benjamin Lee Whorf has shown how the Hopi Indians have a different structure of language from ours which not only influences their thinking, but the very world that they perceive. So Korzybski, a Polish scientist and engineer, was one of the first scholars to emphasize the importance of language as one of the key factors in our thinking, communicating and behaving.

We have often heard the word "environment" referring to those things outside and around us. Korzybski emphasized language as an important part of our environment. He was 30 years ahead of his time and we now find scholars moving in the direction that he speculated upon.

What do we mean by language as an important part of our environment? Our language environment consists of books, newspapers, radio, television, novels, movies and many other forms that create pictures inside of our heads. This is predominantly a verbal environment that creates "meanings" inside of our nervous system. Korzybski called the meanings inside of us our "neuro-semantic environment." "Neuro" refers to our nervous system and "semantic" refers to meanings. For example, whenever we use the words "actor," "actress," "professor," "psychiatrist," "hypnotist," "stage hypnotist," "Catholic," etc., we have "pictures inside of our heads." The pictures inside of our heads are our neurosemantic environment, the meanings inside of our skins. And this is the difference between the older school of "semantics" and "general semantics." Semantics starts with the assumption that meanings are inside of words. General semantics starts with the assumption that meanings are inside of people — which they are. And this is why psychiatry and anthropology are important fields of study to the general semanticist. Meanings are not in words, as we have been taught in our English classes for hundreds of years. Meanings are in our heads, in our nervous systems, in our responses. Words don't mean, people mean, and this is why we have so many misunderstandings in our world today.

In future columns I will give many examples of this. But for now, try to remember that all meanings are personal and unique with you, because no one has lived your particular life. The meanings that you give to words are (may be) different than the meanings that other people give to the same words. Why is this important? Because too often we wrongly assume that other people use words as we do. We therefore wrongly assume that other people mean what we mean. And this is when we have misunderstandings.

Because meanings are in people, and not in words, we cannot eliminate misunderstandings completely. But we can lessen misunderstandings by following some of the principles that will be outlined here. Remember the following:

1. Our language environment creates pictures inside of our heads that may or may not conform to the world of reality.

2. The picture inside of our head is not the world of reality outside of us.

3. When the pictures or meanings inside of us do not conform to the factual world outside of us we have problems.

4. Meanings are not in words, they are inside of people.

5. If you want to lessen misunderstandings, try to find out what people mean, not what words mean.

2
Eliminate spoken misunderstandings

Why do we have misunderstandings? There are many reasons and some of them center around our use or misuse of language.

If you want to lessen misunderstandings you must realize that words are ambiguous; they can have many meanings. People too often wrongly assume that a word has only one meaning, *their* meaning. But words have many meanings, as any large dictionary will point out. Words are not only ambiguous, but people also respond to words differently. The following examples will illustrate how people respond to words.

"Any big men born around here?" a tourist asked in a condescending tone. "Nope," responded the native. "Best we can do is babies. Different in the city, I suppose."

As the conductor called out the various names of the streets, the country couple became more and more uneasy. The conductor called "Maple," then "Adams," and then "Rosewood." The country man grew very fidgety and, turning to his wife said, "Isn't it time we got off?" "Don't show your ignorance, Mathew," she said. "Wait until your name is called."

Several years ago we had a maid living with us by the name of Sylvia. In giving last-minute instructions to Sylvia, my mother, planning a dinner for company, said, "Now, Sylvia, when you serve be sure not to spill anything." "Don't worry," Sylvia said, "I won't say a thing!"

We learn the "meaning of words" from our past experience. A visiting Englishman was greatly confused by American word usage. Complaining to some American friends, he took the word "fix" as an example. "When I am invited to dinner, my host asks me how I would like my drink fixed. He means mixed. My hostess tells me to hurry because dinner is all fixed. She means prepared. My host says he must get his flat tire fixed. And this time he means repaired. You say you are on a fixed income. You mean steady, unchanged. You say you will fix something to the wall. You mean attach. Then you say you'll fix him. And you mean get revenge. Finally, you remark that you're in a devil of a fix. And I see that you may have some comprehension of my predicament in trying to understand your simplified English!"

Many parlor or betting games are based upon the ambiguity of language and each person is "right" according to his own definition of terms. But misunderstandings and arguments result when individuals do not realize that the other person might mean something entirely different.

A track star was boasting of his achievements when a man sitting at a nearby table interrupted him. "I'll race you," said the stranger, "and you'll never pass me if you give me a three-foot start and let me choose the course." The star looked at the portly gentleman and laughed. "Bet you 50 to 1 I will," he returned, "Where's the course?" "Up a ladder," answered the challenger.

If we learn the meanings of words from our past experience, we must realize that meanings are personal. Each person responds to words in a unique, individual manner. For example, a young psychoanalyst was telling an older colleague about his troubles in getting intelligent responses from his patients. "Suppose you ask me some of your questions," the older analyst suggested. "Well, my first question is, 'What is it that wears a skirt and from whose lips come pleasure?'" "A Scot blowing a bagpipe," the veteran answered. "Right," said the younger one. "Now, 'What is it that has smooth curves and at unexpected times becomes uncontrollable?'" "Randy Jones pitching."

"Right!" " 'What do you think of when two arms slip around your shoulder?' " "Why a football tackle," replied the veteran. "Right," said the younger doctor. "All of your answers are amazingly correct. But you'd be surprised at the silly answers I keep getting!"

Meanings are not in the words we use, they are in the minds and the nervous systems of the people using the words. General semantics is a neurological, psychological, anthropological attitude toward meaning. We know from the communication problems that we have had in the United Nations that meanings are not in the words but in the nervous systems of the delegates.

There are international, national, regional and personal differences in the use of language. And we must look for and expect these differences. For example, the Lord's Prayer has had to withstand considerable abuse, especially from children trying to learn it from poor enunciators or from mumbling congregations. One little boy was heard to pray, "Harold be Thy Name." Another begged, "Give us this day our jelly bread." A New York child petitioned, "Lead us not into Penn station."

What is the relationship between language usage and misunderstandings? In our next column we will point out how language usage leads toward misunderstandings and how to lessen them.

3
Bypassing can be a bad word

Language usage contributes toward misunderstandings when we assume that a word has only one meaning — our meaning. We fall victim to this misevaluation because most of us have been brought up in only one language and we think that there is an inherent connection between a word and what it represents. Those who speak several languages know that there are several words to stand for the same object and the relationship between words and things is purely arbitrary. This leads to a further false assumption that meanings are "in" words. But words don't mean anything, people mean. Meanings are in people and their responses, not in words.

Our English teachers must teach this important semantic difference. If you are taught that "words have meaning" you more easily fall victim to projection and misunderstanding — you wrongly project your meaning into others and assume that they mean what you mean. Wrongly projecting your meaning into someone else's words is a common phenomenon, it is the easiest thing in the world to have misunderstandings. Projection and misunderstanding are common occurrences in everyday business.

A woman ordered some writing paper at a department store and asked to have her initials engraved thereon. The salesgirl suggested placing them in the upper right-hand corner or the upper left-hand corner, but the customer said,

"No, put them in the center." The stationery arrived, every sheet marked with her initials equidistant from right and left and from top and bottom.

The speaker means one thing, the listener means something else. This is what we mean by the misevaluation of projection or bypassing, where we wrongly project our meaning into someone else's words and assume that they mean what we mean. Bypassing, as the name implies, means that we are bypassing each other.

There are two important unconscious assumptions that underlie projection or bypassing (misunderstandings). There is an unconscious assumption that others use words as we do. We unconsciously assume that other people mean what we mean. The following example illustrates this kind of misunderstanding.

A motorist swears this story is true. He was driving toward New York when his car stalled. The battery was dead. He flagged a woman driver and she agreed to push his car to get it started. Because his car has an automatic transmission the driver explained, "You'll have to get up to 30 to 35 miles an hour to get me started."

The woman nodded wisely. The driver climbed into his car and waited — and waited. Then he turned around to see where the woman was. She was there all right — coming at him at 30 to 35 miles an hour!

The second unconscious assumption that leads to misunderstandings is the assumption that words have meaning — that meanings are in words. My professor at Northwestern University, Dr. Irving J. Lee, has described this false assumption as the "container myth," the mythical assumption that words contain meaning. William Shakespeare was conscious of this when he said, "A jest's prosperity lies in the ear of him that hears it, never in the tongue of him that makes it."

One of the best examples that I know, to illustrate that meanings are not in words but in our responses, is the following:

"I don't like Bill," confided a coed to her roommate. "He knows too many naughty songs."

"Does he sing them to you?" asked her friend.

"Well, no — but he whistles them!"

If we assume that others use words as we do and that meanings are in words, then it is also easy to assume that others mean what we mean — there is no necessity of asking questions such as "What do you mean?" And people who don't ask questions, whether speakers or listeners, are normally those who have misunderstandings.

Therefore, for effective communication and the lessening of misunderstandings, we must substitute two important conscious assumptions in place of the above two unconscious assumptions that lead toward misunderstandings. We must be conscious of the fact that others do not necessarily mean what we mean, and meanings are in people, not in words. If we are conscious of the above two assumptions, we will adopt a different mode of communication. Our attention will be on the speaker, not his words. We will want to know what the speaker means, not what words mean. We will not be too quick in assuming that others mean what we mean. We will check our assumptions, if necessary, to get on the other person's channel of communication.

Many scholars have long recognized this semantic problem. One of the earliest and greatest semanticists was A.B. Johnson. He said, "Much of what is esteemed as profound philosophy is nothing but a disputatious criticism on the meaning of words." Professor A. Schuster said, "Scientific controversies constantly resolve themselves into differences about the meaning of words." And John Locke observed, "Men content themselves with the same words as other people use, as if the sound necessarily carried the same meaning."

Before you disagree with or misunderstand others, ask them, "What do you mean?" or, "Is this what you wanted me to do?" If you are a speaker, invite the listener to get on your channel of communication. The burden for effective communication is upon both the speaker and the listener. Each has an important job to do if we are to lessen misunderstandings.

4
Communication is the key

When I was teaching general semantics and effective communication at the University of Chicago and Northwestern University I often got into discussions on the importance of communication in business and educational courses. I felt that many people did not realize how important communication is.

I was pleasantly surprised when I later met an old friend, a philosophy professor, who immediately remarked, "You know, you certainly are in the right field. Everywhere you go you hear people in business and education talking about communication."

This professor had been most critical of general semantics and the emphasis on communication in earlier books and discussions. As most people are when others agree with them, I was happy to see that this heretofore critical professor had finally seen the light.

Almost all the executives that I lecture to or come in contact with agree that communication is one of the most important areas in business and industry and that their job involves communication, in one way or another, 85 or 90 percent of the time. And yet, there are dreadfully few courses on communication in the schools of business and industrial relations centers at our leading colleges or universities. I am not talking about courses in public speaking or letter writing. While these courses are important, I am referring to the kind of day-to-day communication in business and industry, on the job and off the job, that we are continually engaged in.

There are some general communication principles that apply to all kinds of communication and which are related to the scientific method. These are general principles that can be applied to human communication.

The first, and one of the most important is the need to pause, delay and analyze in our communicating and behavior. Many misunderstandings and disagreements result from an automatic, trigger-like response to someone else's words or behavior. If we could but pause and delay a little longer than we normally do — a two-second activity delay — we would not have some of the arguments and disagreements in which we find ourselves.

The problem of misunderstanding is one of the most common and pernicious. The amount of time and money that is wasted due to misunderstandings and otherwise poor communication is difficult to estimate. But it is enormous indeed. Why do people have misunderstandings? There are many reasons, of course, but let us mention just a few.

One of the causes is the unconscious assumption on the part of the speaker that the listener understands him. He, therefore, fails to aid the listener in getting on his (the speaker's) channel of communication by asking him if he understands.

Listeners, too, unconsciously assume that they understand the speaker. They fail to ask the speaker, "What do you mean?" or "Jane, is this what you meant, or want me to do?"

There are two unconscious assumptions here that lead to misunderstanding. First, we unconsciously assume that others use words as we do, that others mean what we would mean if we were doing the talking. Second, we assume that meanings are in words, that words contain meaning. But words don't mean — PEOPLE mean. Meanings are not in words, they are in people. As the famous philosopher Charles Sanders Peirce said, "You do not get meaning, you respond with meaning."

There is one last assumption that is, perhaps, the most unfortunate of all and is a major cause of such poor communication that we find today. This is the assumption that we don't need to improve our communication. Although most people, especially executives, admit the importance of communication, some of them do not really feel it to be important, or they feel that they do not need to improve their own communication. These tend to be the ones who need it the most.

So, the first problem in communication is getting people to realize — to really believe — that it is an important problem. Only then are they ready to improve their communicating, to work on themselves. For, improvement does not come from without, but from within.

5

The problem of communication

I started another Effective Communication and Success Motivation Seminar and of the several newspaper ads that we had, most contained wrong information. In other words, in the process of communication, someone made an error or a mistake. This is nothing new, either in the newspaper profession or in any other business. Mistakes, errors and communication failures run rampant in all areas where human beings are involved.

As a teacher of general semantics and effective communication for the past 25 years I have always been concerned with several things relative to this problem of communications. One is the fact that while communication is the No. 1 problem in business and industry, as well as in life, few people believe that they need to take courses to improve their own communication. In other words, it's the other person's fault!

As a management and communication consultant, I have noticed that many top executives look upon a communication course as a kind of "frill," something that their management or workers can get a lecture on, but nothing that really needs an entire course.

The tragedy in education, especially relative to communication and success motivation, is that the ones who need this kind of training the most are never in your classes. They somehow feel that this is for other people. And yet they are the problems in business and industry, as well as at home. These are the ones with a negative mental attitude. These are the ones with a closed mind. In general semantics we call this an "allness" orientation, the assumption that we know it all, the disease of "psychological arteriosclerosis," a kind of hardening of the attitudes!

And out of those who do attend these classes, perhaps 10 percent of your students are unable to get on your channel of communication. You can see it in their faces, you can see it in their bodily communication. This is called "kinesics," body language or non-verbal communication. And while you cannot get to these 10 percent, they are the ones who need this training the most. When they listen to your lecture, they don't hear what you are saying. They are only listening to themselves. They make up their minds too quickly, in a negative manner. They jump to conclusions too readily. They wrongly project meaning into your words, meanings that you did not have in the first place. Usually this small percentage of students will drop out, and here is the tragedy, because these are precisely the problems that you will be lecturing on.

Why do we make these communication errors, misunderstandings and mistakes in business, industry and in life?

1. We wrongly assume that meanings are in words. We are taught this in high schools and colleges. But words don't mean anything. People mean! Meanings are in speakers and in listeners and the burden in effective communication is upon both the speaker and the listener. If you are not sure, ask the speaker, "What do you mean?"

2. We react too quickly in communication and in life generally. We make snap judgments. We have too many impulsive reactions. We don't take the time to allow the cortex (the "thinking" part of the brain that allows us to see differences) to play the human role in our behavior. Most of our behavior is animal-like, impulsive and trigger-like. We must learn to pause, delay, and analyze situations intelligently in terms of facts, not in terms of false assumptions.

3. We jump to conclusions because we have never been taught the difference between a factual statement and an

inference or an assumption. We are unscientific in our behavior because we have never been taught that there is a scientific method for everyday human behavior, just as there is in the laboratory.

4. We close our minds because we are creatures of habit, negative habits, and don't realize that we can change these negative habits into positive ones. Changing habits is always difficult. It takes time, energy and hard work.

5. Asking questions is the best method to overcome mistakes and communication problems. If you are not sure, ask the other person. Before you make a mistake, and cost your company hundreds or thousands of dollars, check your inferences or assumptions with the person who gave you the directive. And he may very well have to check his information with the person who gave him the information. Asking the right questions of other people, as well as of ourselves, is the quickest way toward sane behavior and the lessening of communication problems.

MAKING ASSUMPTIONS AND JUMPING TO CONCLUSIONS

6
Dangers lurking in our assumptions

As a teacher of general semantics and effective communications for the past 25 years, I have been continually aware of the many kinds of thinking and communication errors that people make, myself included. In general semantics we call them misevaluations. When our thinking, communicating, and behaving do not fit the world of reality, we are misevaluating.

All behavior of man (and animals) can be defined in terms of proper or misevaluations. A proper evaluation is an evaluation that fits the facts and, therefore, we call it "intelligent." A misevaluation is an evaluation that does not fit the facts and which we might call "stupid" or "immature." The following is a good example of a person who, although the world of reality changes, refuses to change his way of thinking to fit the facts.

During a heavy flood a little girl was perched on top of a house with a small boy. As they watched articles float along they noticed a derby hat on the water. Presently the hat turned and came back, then turned again and went downstream. After it went away downstream, it turned and came back again.

The little girl said: "Did you see that derby? First it goes downstream, then it turns and comes back."

The boy replied: "Oh, that's my father. He said, 'Come hell or high water, I'm going to cut the grass today!' "

How many of us refuse to change our ways of thinking to fit the changing facts? How many of us behave stupidly because of certain false assumptions about ourselves, others, or the very language that we use.

Two of my favorite words are "ignorance" and "stupidity." Ignorance is merely lack of knowledge and all of us are ignorant in all areas. We cannot know "all" about anything, so vast is the knowledge in any field of study. But "stupidity" is something else again. We behave stupidly when we think that we know it all. We behave stupidly when we presume to have knowledge that we don't have. We behave stupidly when we jump to conclusions. These and many other kinds of misevaluations will be analyzed here, and we will give you some pointers on how to behave intelligently and scientifically in an unintelligent world.

Just take a look at the newspapers, and around you, and you will find plenty of examples of stupidity at work. All of the fights, arguments, disagreements and errors that people make are testimony to the unscientific behavior that is a characteristic of "rational man."

When Alfred Korzybski used to lecture on Aristotle's definition of man as a "rational animal," he used to thunder in his Polish accent, "Oh yeah, vere da hell is it?" He knew that there are too many examples of irrational behavior in rational man.

And so we will present some prescriptions for rationality in an irrational world.

One of the reasons why we have misevaluations is that we make certain false assumptions, and they are usually on the unconscious level. These false unconscious assumptions lead toward thinking, communicating, and behavior errors or problems. We do not say that you should not make assumptions, for you must make assumptions. But wisdom begins when you are conscious of some of the assumptions that you are making.

It's impossible not to make assumptions. For example, you are assuming that the chair you are sitting on will hold you. I am assuming that you are sitting. It is impossible not to make assumptions, as indicated in the following example.

24

In California a psychiatric patient was asked if he were Napoleon. He craftily said, "No." A lie detector showed that he was lying.

Why are our unconscious assumptions important in our thinking, communicating and behaving? Let me give you just a few of the many reasons:

1. If you assume that other people don't like you, they won't. We will write more about self-fulfilling prophecies and how your assumptions about others create the same reaction toward you.

2. If you assume that meanings are in words, rather than in people, you don't ask other people, "What do you mean?" because you assume you know what they mean, because you *know* what the words mean. But what words mean to you and to others can be two entirely different things.

3. If you assume that you know it all you fall victim to the disease of "psychological arteriosclerosis." This leads toward the closed mind and psychological rigidity.

Quote for the day: When we assume too much, this is how you spell it, ASS-U-ME — it makes an ass of you and me!

7

Perils of assumption

It shook me up for two days. I had stopped at an intersection, ready to make a left turn. All of a sudden I saw a young man on a bicycle shoot out in front of me trying to miss a car in front of him, only to swerve left, right into the path of an oncoming car. He hit head-on, was tossed into the air along with his bicycle, crumpling to the street. I was surprised at how fast he was going, seemingly unaware of the assumptions of the people driving around him, or of his own.

It was terrible to see but it made me think of the many people who are totally unaware of their own and others' unconscious assumptions. When we drive our automobiles, bicycles, motorcycles, trucks, buses, and other forms of transportation, we all make many assumptions of which we are unaware.

Too many of us drive too quickly and assume that the brakes will hold. When we go to pass another car we look into the rear-view mirror and pull to the left to pass, only to be surprised that there is another car to our left. Too many people act first and then look, whereas they should look first and then act.

For 15 years I taught general semantics and safety at the Traffic Institute at Northwestern University. We were concerned with the causes of accidents. Most accidents are caused by human error, not mechanical failure. And the most important parts of human error are our unconscious assumptions.

Most of us drive our cars as animals would. Let me explain what I mean from the point of view of general semantics. There are two ways of responding to a traffic light. We are taught or conditioned that a green light means go and a red light means stop.

We can train a chimpanzee or an animal to go at a green light and stop at a red light. These are conditioned responses. To an animal it IS "go" or "stop," it is a *signal*.

To a human, however, it should be a *symbol* rather than a *signal*. A symbol is that which represents or stands for something else. The green light or red light means go or stop — MAYBE. It all depends upon the traffic situation.

As has been mentioned, human beings are the only ones who are capable of reacting with higher degrees of *conditionality*. They are the only ones, who, potentially, are able to pause, delay, analyze, and observe in the presence of symbols such as red and green lights. Because of this symbol reaction they can make their thinking and behavior fit the facts.

Some automobile drivers drive as if the green light ALWAYS means go. It means go MAYBE. It doesn't mean go if a child runs in front of your car. The facts of the situation, not the light, must control your behavior. You must be more aware, you must have reactions with a higher degree of conditionality, rather than the automatic, conditioned responses.

Once when I was explaining this principle to a group of executives in San Francisco one of the students disagreed. He said, "Do you mean to tell me that if I hear the telephone ring, I shouldn't automatically reach for it right away?" I was trying to explain the important point that external suggestions should not control our behavior, we must learn to control our own responses.

In giving my answer to the business executive I paused, delayed, and analyzed, trying to have a conditional response myself. He thought that he had me, because anyone knows that if the phone rings you should automatically pick it up. I answered, "How about if you are at your friend's house?"

The other students laughed and realized that there is great danger in having an automatic, conditioned response like animals.

Life is a series of unconscious assumptions. And the quicker we realize this the more sane our behavior will be. Not only in driving our cars but in all of our interpersonal relationships. Assumptions are not factual. They are inferences. Assumptions should be checked.

8
What do you assume?

One of the most important questions that we can ask ourselves is, "What am I assuming when I am thinking, talking and behaving?" When we are speaking, listening, thinking, observing, behaving, what assumptions are we making? Our unconscious assumptions control our behavior.

Life is a series of unconscious assumptions. We must make assumptions. But wisdom begins when we are conscious of some of the assumptions that we make.

We can say one thing, but what we really mean is something else again. Our unconscious assumptions indicate how we really feel about things.

It is important to remember that we speak, think, observe and behave according to the unconscious assumptions that we make about people, situations, things, and most importantly, about ourselves.

Voltaire was conscious of this in the course of an argument. A question was brought up and he said, "There are too many of us present." The other replied, "What do you mean? There are only two of us present."

Voltaire said, "I'm sure that there are at least six of us. There is what you are, what you think you are and what I think you are. And there is what I am, what I think I am, and what you think I am."

What we think about ourselves, the picture that we have of ourselves, is due to these unconscious assumptions. What you think you are is not you. It is an abstraction or a map of the "real self." This phenomenon self, what you think you are or the way you would like to look to yourself, is a product of the assumptions that you make about yourself. The important thing in effective communication and good mental health is to understand these assumptions as much as we can and to try to bring this self-concept to reality. This is what we mean by maturity.

From our set of assumptions or premises our feelings and behavior logically follow. This is what mathematician-philosopher Cassius Keyser called logical fate or logical destiny. From our unconscious assumptions our conclusions or behavior logically follow.

We tend to overlook the fact that assuming-feeling-thinking-behaving are part of a single act. If we have an unconscious assumption that we "know it all," don't be surprised if we have attitudes, feelings and behavior of the know-it-all and closed mind. The "know-it-all attitude" or assumption does not fit the structure of the world of reality for no one can know all about anything. The world is extremely complex and unlimited while our knowledge must, of necessity, be limited.

And so we are concerned with the kinds of assumptions that "fit the structure of the world of reality," that fit the facts, that are mature, efficient, productive, and lead toward a high degree of predictability. This is the basis of general semantics and the scientific method. For it is impossible not to have assumptions as indicated in the following examples:

During a heated campaign in Cincinnati over fluoridation of the water supply, a woman called "The Enquirer" to say that she didn't vote for fluoridation because she felt it wasn't anything for the average citizen to decide. "So," she declared, "I voted against it!"

"I'm against Kennedy," said one retired Atlanta railroad engineer, "but I'm not going to explain why. You might be a Catholic."

A young father was telling a group of friends what a bad time he had when his baby was born. Finally a young matron inquired: "Who had that baby, anyway?"

The young man nodded toward his wife, "She did," he answered quite seriously. "But she had an anesthetic."

Try to dig out some of the unconscious assumptions that stand in the way of your effective communication, good human relations, a happy marriage, or a successful life. What false assumptions do you have about yourself or others that are holding you back? If you have difficulty understanding some of these false assumptions perhaps a good psychologist or psychiatrist can help. After all, this is his or her job, digging out false assumptions that people have about themselves that get in the way of productive and happy living. And then people can do something about those false assumptions.

We project our unconscious assumptions onto the world of reality. We are both the creator and the product of our assumptions.

9
Learning to control response

In my last column I wrote about the problem of communication. Now let us take a closer look at why we have so many communication and human relations problems at home, on the job, and in life generally.

One of the main reasons we jump to conclusions or have misunderstandings is that we tend to have impulsive, trigger-like reactions. Let us analyze three different kinds of responses to see what a human kind of response is like.

1. A reflex action is inborn, not conditioned or learned. If you shine a light into the pupil of your eye, it will constrict or close. Hit the patellar tendon of the knee and your knee jerks. Hit the plantar tendon on the base of the foot and you get an immediate response. These are reflex actions, quick, immediate, automatic, trigger-like responses, where the stimulus controls the response. There is not much that we can do about reflex actions as they are not conditioned or learned.

2. A signal reaction is reflex-like behavior. It, too, is quick, automatic, trigger-like, impulsive, but it is learned or conditioned. You and I have learned how to respond in an automatic, quick, unthinking manner and here too the stimulus controls the response. Too much of our behavior is thus rigid, habitual, unchanging, although the world of reality changes. A signal reaction is learned or conditioned. Therefore, we can unlearn signal reactions. We can stop

behaving like emotionally disturbed persons or people with primitive mentality.

Psychiatrist Dr. S.H. Kraines, in his book, *Managing Your Mind,* spends almost half of the book describing how patients with emotional or mental problems respond in an impulsive manner. He also stresses the necessity of pausing and delaying one's response in order to achieve maturity. Anthropologists have pointed out that modern man did not become modern man until he stopped to think, until he paused, delayed and analyzed situations, in order to have a more human kind of response. It is a delayed response that makes one human.

3. This third kind of response is called a symbol reaction. Alfred Korzybski, the father of general semantics, in his book, *Science and Sanity,* pointed out the important difference between signal reactions and symbol reactions. Signal reactions are quick, impulsive, automatic responses, controlled by the stimulus. Some of you might recall the reactions to an Orson Welles broadcast in 1938. These were a series of unthinking, signal reactions. Panic behavior is characteristic of signal reactions. Mature behavior is characteristic of symbol reactions.

While animals' responses are conditioned, human responses are capable of having a higher degree of conditionality. This means that they can change their responses, depending upon the facts of the situation. Conditioned responses are animalistic responses. They are the same no matter what the external facts are. This is why rat traps are so effective to catch rats. To a rat, "cheese is cheese." I suggest, however, that cheese inside of a rat trap is not quite the same as cheese outside of a rat trap. To a fish, "minnow is minnow," but one at the end of a hook is not quite the same as a minnow not at the end of a hook.

How many of us have the same kind of automatic, conditioned responses to people, situations and things? We have these "frozen" responses, as if the world of reality or the people in it never change. How can we learn the symbol reaction, the human kind of response, in our dealings with people?

We can learn how to pause, delay, analyze situations more than we normally do.

In pausing and delaying, and allowing the cortex to "think" and see differences, we are behaving like humans rather than animals. We are not lowering ourselves to an animalistic kind of response. We are not CATegorists or DOGmatists.

By having a symbol reaction, we control the situation or response, rather than having the stimulus or external event control us. Self-control is one of the most important of human responses.

By having a symbol reaction our behavior becomes much more mature. In fact, this is what we mean by mature behavior, being able to control ourselves, being able to analyze situations objectively.

Signal reactions lead toward many other kinds of mis-evaluations, arguments, fights and disagreements. In future columns we will analyze the different kinds of misevaluations that signal reactions lead into. For now, however, if you remember that symbol reactions are a human kind of response, you will tend to pause, delaying and analyzing situations, rather than "bursting out into speech" or "flying off the handle."

Quote for the day: The purpose which runs through all other educational purposes — the common thread of education — is the development of the ability to think. — *Educational Policies Commission.*

10
Differentiating — fact and inference

In our last column we talked about how our automatic, trigger-like reactions lead toward misevaluations. One of the most common kinds of misevaluations is jumping to conclusions. Why do we jump to conclusions? One of the important reasons that we jump to conclusions is that we have never been taught the difference between a statement of fact and a statement involving an inference, an assumption, or a guess.

In my book, *Why Do We Jump to Conclusions?* I point out five differentiating characteristics between a statement of fact and an inferential statement. First, a factual statement can only be made after you have observed something, whereas an inference can be made anytime — before, during or after observation, or, as is usually the case, with no observation at all. In other words, unless you have seen something with your own eyes, you are speaking inferentially.

Second, a statement of fact stays with what can be observed, whereas an inferential statement goes beyond observation. The following example illustrates how easy it is to jump to conclusions or make false inferences.

My mother rented a room in our house to two boys whom she did not know. She was a little worried at first, but in a few days she stopped fretting. "They must be nice boys," she explained. "They have towels from the YMCA."

Whenever I ask my students to make a statement of fact about the above story, some say, "The boys stole the towels" or "They took the towels from the YMCA." These statements are obviously inferential. They go beyond the facts. If they say, "The boys have towels with YMCA printed on them," they stay within what my mother observed.

A third differentiating feature between a statement of fact and one that is inferential is that a statement of fact approaches certainty whereas statements involving an inference have varying degrees of probability. Why don't we say that a statement of fact is certain? Heisenberg's principle of indeterminacy (or uncertainty principle) states that the moment we talk about the world of reality we are in the realm of probability.

In other words, our statements and behavior are probable, not certain. Too many of us, however, jump to conclusions. We are too certain about what other people mean or do. We fail to ask questions. We are certain that we know what other people mean, when we don't. This is why we have misunderstandings. When we are too certain, we don't ask questions or check our assumptions. This is important in scientific behavior. You must replace your assumptions of certainty with assumptions of probability.

A fourth characteristic of a statement of fact is that we can make a limited number of factual statements but an unlimited number of inferences. It is the easiest thing in the world to make inferences. It takes no grey matter or intelligence to jump to conclusions. As someone once said, "Jumping to conclusions is the poorest form of exercise." But knowing the difference between our inferences and statements of fact is the beginning of wisdom.

A fifth characteristic difference between a factual statement and an inferential statement is that factual statements tend to lead to agreement whereas inferential statements lead to disagreement. There is so much disagreement in the political arena because so much of the discussion or argument is inferential, rather than factual.

How can you become more scientific or stop jumping to conclusions?

1. Basically, life is lived on the inferential level. Most of what you and I do is purely inferential. We live in the realm of inferences and assumptions. Make all the inferences you want, but know that you are doing so. Know the difference between your inferences or assumptions and statements of fact.

2. Check your inferences. Scientists make many inferences, some of which are called hypotheses, but they keep testing and checking their inferences. You should do the same in your behavior.

3. Don't pass off inferences as if they were statements of fact. And don't accept others' inferences as if they were factual.

4. Don't act on inferences as if they were factual. Fights, arguments, wars, divorces, are all caused by people acting on inferences as if they were factual. People who jump to conclusions often wrongly accuse others of behavior that they were not guilty of.

5. Orient your life in terms of the "assumptions of probability," not the "assumptions of certainty." Don't be too certain. The person who is certain never checks his assumptions or inferences. He is certain, and he is often wrong.

In our next column, we will apply this principle to the newspaper profession, a profession that deals in words all of the time.

Quote for the day: The question is not whether or not we make inferences; the question is whether or not we are aware of the inferences we make. — *S.I. Hayakawa.*

11
Delaying jumps to conclusions

In our last column we differentiated between a factual statement and an inferential statement. We said that a statement of fact can only be made after observation, and stays with what has been observed, whereas an inference can be made at anytime and goes beyond observation. For example, if you observe a table in your room, that table is the non-verbal fact. If you say, "This table is in the room," that is a statement of fact. Notice that facts are non-verbal and statements are verbal. If you read a label on the back of the table that says, "G.B. Clark Company, Los Angeles, California," and if you say, "This table was manufactured in Los Angeles, California," that is an inference. You don't know where it was manufactured. If you have observed the label all that you can factually say is, "The label says G.B. Clark Company, Los Angeles, California."

Why is this so important? Because we all continually jump to conclusions. People make inferences and false assumptions and think that they are uttering factual statements. Divorces and unhappy human relations are centered around people making false accusations and attributing motives to others that are only within themselves.

Notice how often people have opinions about others that they don't even know. They base their opinions on the flimsiest of evidence. This is why I tell my students, "Never criticize anyone until you know why they are doing what they are doing, from their point of view." We have many people who continually knock others, basically because they are unhappy with their own lot in life. And this is precisely why they have never achieved very much, because they are filled with hate and a negative mental attitude.

Psychiatrists say that people who hate others basically hate themselves. Those who are envious, cynical, jealous, or negative, are merely projecting their own internal state onto the world around them. Self-hate is the greatest disease that man has.

Too many people have bad opinions about themselves. And notice that I said "opinion." Unfortunately, these individuals act as if these negative opinions are facts. And so they create these negative opinions into non-verbal facts.

Perhaps the most important area for inferences is in newspapers. People read the newspapers as if they are receiving statements of fact when in reality the ability of the reader to verify or corroborate what they read is practically zero. The reader must assume that what the writer is describing is a factual statement, which immediately puts the reader on the inferential level. Let me describe this in terms of three different levels of abstracting.

Alfred Korzybski described at least three different orders of abstraction in his book, *Science and Sanity.* If you see a fire, that is a first-order abstraction. You are abstracting, or selecting directly from the non-verbal fact. If you say, "I see a fire" or "The fire burned down the buildings," that is a statement about the non-verbal fact. The statement is one order removed from the actual observation, so that is a second-order abstraction. And if a newspaper reporter writes about the burning building, that is a third-order abstraction to the newspaper reader — the reader is further removed from the actual happening.

This shows you how newspaper reporters can introduce inferences, opinions, or assumptions into their writing, but especially why the reader is, of necessity, continually on the inferential, rather than the factual level. This is why we are often surprised when we read about a person in a newspaper or magazine, and when we meet them personally they turn out to be completely different than the "picture inside of our head." The "picture inside of our head" is never the fact; it is an opinion, an assumption, at best a guess.

This means that we should hold our opinions tentatively and be willing to change them the moment the facts indicate that we should. Newspapers are one of the most important means of information and education. But we must remember that words, and words about words, and words about words about other people's words, are never the direct experience. This is what we mean by the inferential level.

Make all of the inferences that you want, but know that you are doing so. Know the difference between your statements of fact and your inferences or assumptions.

Be intelligently critical (but open-minded) about your language environment (newspapers, radio, television, magazines, etc.) Don't accept everything that you read as factual (including this column). See if it works for you. Intelligent skepticism, said Bertrand Russell, is the beginning of intelligent behavior. Knowing the difference between false assumptions and facts is the beginning of wisdom, intelligence, maturity, or scientific behavior.

PROBLEMS WITH
THE CLOSED MIND

12
Our human limitations

Whenever I ask my students, "Can we ever know 'all' about anything?" they invariably answer "no." The more we discuss anything the more we realize how little we can know about it. There are vast ramifications and relationships to everything. Then I ask them, "Have you ever met individuals who act as if they know 'all' about something?" and there is usually a thunderous "yes."

Why can't we know all about anything? What are the limitations of our acquaintance with anything?

Time is an important limiting factor. We only have a limited amount of time to observe something. This is usually very short. In our everyday observations we have but a fleeting second to observe the world of reality, hardly enough to "know all about it."

Space is another important limiting factor. We all observe the world of reality from different physical points of view. There is no physical position that will give us full focus on all aspects of a thing. Look at any object and you must, of necessity, abstract some characteristics and eliminate others.

Complexity is another limiting factor. The world of reality is complex but too often some people want simple solutions to problems. To unlock the secret of atomic energy, or to send a man to the moon, required the work of many scientists all over the world for many generations. The man in the street is frequently accused of dealing in half truths, but where is the whole truth to be found?

William Jennings Bryan had this to say to those who were continually looking for the simple answers: "Let him find out, if he can, why it is that a black cow can eat green grass and then give white milk with yellow butter in it."

Interest is another limiting variable. What interests one person does not necessarily interest someone else. What we are interested in will indicate what we abstract or select from the world of reality. For example, two medical specialists were off on a holiday: "These girls in Florida certainly have beautiful legs, don't they?" said the orthopedist, after an appreciative look around the beach. "I hadn't noticed," said his companion. "I'm a chest man, myself." We see things not as they are but as we are.

Position or space is another limiting factor. We see things from a particular point of view. Alfred Korzybski, in an article called "The Role of Language in the Perceptual Process" shows how darkness influenced four different abstractions from one situation. He wrote, "In a railroad compartment an American grandmother with her young and attractive granddaughter, a Romanian officer, and a Nazi officer were the only occupants. The train was passing through a dark tunnel, and all that was heard was a loud kiss and a vigorous slap. After the train emerged from the tunnel, nobody spoke, but the grandmother was saying to herself, "What a fine girl I have raised. She will take care of herself. I am proud of her." The granddaughter was saying to herself, "Well, grandmother is old enough not to mind a little kiss. Besides, the fellows are nice. I am surprised what a hard wallop grandmother has." The Nazi officer was meditating, "How clever those Romanians are! They steal a kiss and have the other fellow slapped." The Romanian officer was chuckling to himself, "How smart I am! I kissed my own hand and slapped the Nazi."

There are many other limiting factors of our acquaintance with things.

Language is an important variable in thinking, perceiving, communicating and behaving. This is one of the important principles in general semantics. The title of Korzybski's above article implies the relationship between language and human perception. Anthropologists and linguists such as Edward Sapir and Benjamin Lee Whorf, along with Korzybski, have emphasized the important role that language plays in thinking, perceiving and behaving.

We could list the limiting factors of our acquaintance with things almost indefinitely. There are sex differences. There are sense limitations or limitations of our nervous system. Education, training and culture are important variables in why we see things as we do. Religion is an extremely important variable and many wars have been fought because of it, and are still being fought today.

Why is it important to recognize the limiting factors of our acquaintance with things? When we fail to realize that we can only abstract or select a small amount of any total situation, we think we know it all. These limiting factors indicate that our perception or understanding of anything must, of necessity, be partial and, therefore, we cannot know all about anything.

The person who thinks he or she knows it all is a problem on the job, in a family, as a parent, as a daughter or son, as an executive, in all walks of life. Realizing that we do not know it all makes us much easier to teach, we listen to the points of view of others, we are easier to work and live with.

In our next column we will discuss how to lessen this "allness" orientation, the assumption that we know it all. Wendell Johnson described this psychological disease best when he said, "An attitude of this kind — 'You can't tell me anything about that' — has an effect quite similar to that of a pus sac in the brain."

13
Closed mind blocks learning

In our last column we indicated why we cannot know "all" about anything. But how often have we seen individuals who act as if they know all about something? The assumption that we know it all is called an "allness orientation." The most important thing about the allness orientation is that it afflicts all of us in a very subtle way. What are some of the manifestations of the allness orientation?

1. The Closed Mind. This indicates the refusal to change one's way of thinking in spite of the facts. The closed mind is one of the most prevalent of thinking errors. The tragedy about the closed mind is that many people have a closed mind about those things of which they are the most ignorant.

2. Refusal to learn. One of the most unfortunate manifestations of the allness orientation is the refusal to learn. The greatest tragedy in education is that some students approach a learning situation with a negative mental attitude. Some of our brightest students are not graduating from high school or going to college because of this most important attitude.

The problem in education is not that students or adults cannot learn. The problem is that some students come to class with the attitude, "Show me something I don't already know!" Too many of us come to situations, learning or otherwise, with these kinds of prejudgments (prejudices) that get in the way of our learning or understanding. We make up our minds too quickly. We jump to conclusions too readily. We do not know how to manifest the "uncommon sense" of pausing, delaying and saying, "I don't know. Let's see." Teachers, executives, parents — almost all of us are concerned with the problem of teachability. What makes a person teachable, open to new ideas? What allows a person to change, adapt, or keep up to date?

Epictetus said, "It is impossible for anyone to begin to learn what he thinks he already knows."

3. Refusal to listen. Another way in which the allness orientation appears is in the refusal to listen. We find this "semantic blockage" between husbands and wives, labor and management, parent and child, in many segments of society. Sometimes we set up an "allness" barrier to communication that is hard to penetrate. Because we assume "we know it all," we don't or won't listen.

4. Refusal to change or keep up to date. Ultimately our survival depends upon our keeping up to date. There are many areas where the refusal to change results in humor, irony, or tragedy: the 55-year-old "girl" who acts as if she were 16; the parents of an adult who treat the person as if he or she were still a child; the president of a company who refuses to change the policies of the company to fit the changing facts; nations with the "Maginot Line mentality" who are convinced of their own invincibility. France found out what this kind of thinking can do to a nation.

5. Assuming knowledge that one doesn't have. When we presume to have knowledge that we don't really have, we refuse to ask questions, we refuse to look for the facts. To presume to have knowledge that we don't really have is an easy way of compensating for our feelings of intellectual inadequacy. This is a good way of not appearing "stupid."

Actually, however, we are compounding our ignorance with stupidity. We behave "stupidly" when we presume to have knowledge that we don't have and refuse to ask questions.

To lack knowledge is one thing. But not to recognize our ignorance is something else again. The arrogance of the scholar often looks like humility compared with the arrogance of the ignorant man. "Nothing is so sure of itself as ignorance," said Ludwig Lewisohn. William Shakespeare said, "Man, proud man, dressed in a little brief authority, most ignorant of what he's most assured."

6. Jehovah complex. The "know-it-all" is another man-ifestation of the allness orientation, usually resulting in generalized dogmatic behavior. Dogmatism can be seen in many ways and reminds us of the result gotten by the man who crossed a tiger with a parrot. His friend asked him, "Well, what did you get?" "I don't know," replied the other, "but when he talks, we listen!"

Quote for the day: Some minds are like concrete, all mixed up and permanently set. — *Charles Kettering.*

14
Flexibility — a big plus

One of the problems with many individuals is that they are too rigid; they are unable to change with the changing world of reality. Psychological rigidity is the opposite of flexibility. Of all the skills that we need to develop in order to cope with the variability and change in life, flexibility is one of the most important. But too often individuals have a "closed mind." They refuse to change their ways of thinking to fit the changing facts.

Some people have what the general semanticist calls a "one-valued orientation" — this is the ONLY way to do it or solve the problem. A "multi-valued orientation" is when we realize that there are other answers or ways to solve a problem. Flexibility is the realization that there are alternative solutions to problems, as well as the ability to discard one solution if it doesn't work and select another.

Unfortunately, too many individuals have a sort of built-in rigidity. They feel comfortable doing things the way they have always done them. Man is a creature of habit — even if the habitual behavior is wrong or has outlived its usefulness.

Most people do not understand this idea of flexibility. Too often we look upon the flexible person as a weak person. Flexibility is too closely identified with vacillating. We think that it goes hand-in-hand with an inability to make up our minds. Nothing could be further from the truth. Flexibility makes us realize that facts do change, people change, situations change, and our thinking and behavior must reflect the changing world of reality.

The flexible person is coping creatively. He is intelligent enough to recognize a dead end when he sees one and to seek an alternative solution. He is able to shift gears or change his approach when things aren't working out.

One of the most important lessons to be learned from this flexibility approach is that it not only tells one when to stop trying and change his approach, but also when to keep trying — when he has a realistic chance of success. Too many people keep bumping their nose up against a stone wall and then quit, without trying to change their approach to something that might succeed.

In the 1870s a bishop who had charge of a small denominational college made his annual visit and stayed with the college president. The bishop boasted a firm belief that everything that could be invented had been invented. The college president thought otherwise.

"In 50 years," he said, "men will learn to fly like birds." The bishop, shocked, replied, "Flight is reserved for angels and you have been guilty of blasphemy."

The name of the bishop was Milton Wright, and back home he had two small sons — Orville and Wilbur.

15

We can be
too certain

One of the reasons we have so many problems is that we are too certain in our thinking, communicating and behaving. We don't stop to check our inferences or assumptions. We act as if they are true.

In my classes I make an important distinction between the assumptions of probability and the assumptions of certainty. With our assumptions of certainty we are certain that such and such has happened or will happen. With the assumptions of probability we say, "I don't know. Let's see."

Albert Einstein in his book *Sidelights on Relativity* has said that, "As far as the laws of mathematics refer to reality, they are not certain; and as far as they are certain, they do not refer to reality." The moment we talk about the world of reality we are in the world of probability, not certainty.

If our assumptions or evaluations are going to fit the facts, fit the structure of the world of "reality" at the latest date, we must orient our lives in terms of the assumptions of probability rather than the assumptions of certainty. It is this "assumption of certainty" that leads toward the jumping to conclusions, such as in the following example:

When a jealous husband found a man's billfold in his car, he immediately drove to the address shown on an identification card in the wallet. He rang the bell and, when a man answered, gave him a sound thrashing and a warning. Monday, the husband was fined and given a suspended

30-day jail sentence in municipal court. The owner of the billfold had moved from the address on his identification card.

Notice the assumption of certainty underlying this kind of behavior. How easy it is to assume knowledge that one does not have.

When we orient our lives in terms of the assumptions of certainty, we assume more knowledge than we really have. We do not realize the limitations of our knowledge. Philosopher-mathematician Bertrand Russell presents the certainty problem in the following way. In his book, *Unpopular Essays*, Russell says, "The demand for certainty is one which is natural to man, but is nevertheless an intellectual vice. If you take your children for a picnic on a doubtful day, they will demand a dogmatic answer as to whether it will be fine or wet, and be disappointed in you when you cannot be sure. The same sort of assurance is demanded, in later life, of those who undertake to lead populations into the Promised Land. 'Liquidate the capitalists and the survivors will enjoy eternal bliss.' 'Kill the Croats and let the Serbs reign.' These are examples of the slogans that have won wide popular acceptance in our time.

"Even a modicum of philosophy would make it impossible to accept such bloodthirsty nonsense. But so long as men are not trained to withhold judgment in the absence of evidence, they will be led astray by cocksure prophets, and it is likely that their leaders will be either ignorant fanatics or dishonest charlatans. To endure uncertainty is difficult, but so are most of the other virtues. For the learning of every virtue there is an appropriate discipline, and for the learning of suspended judgment the best discipline is philosophy.

"But if philosophy is to serve a positive purpose, it must not teach mere skepticism, for, while the dogmatist is harmful, the skeptic is useless. Dogmatism and skepticism are both, in a sense, absolute philosophies; one is certain of knowing, the other of not knowing. What philosophy should dissipate is certainty, whether of knowledge, or of ignorance."

If certainty is impossible to attain in a scientific world of reality, then the assumptions of certainty must be discarded, except in mathematics and deductive logic. In a world of uncertainty and indeterminacy, the assumptions of probability fit the structure of the world of reality as we know it today.

We must continually question facts, the adequacy of our decisions, and search for more variables in situations. We should not be more certain in our behavior than the facts call for.

The complete believer, or the person who believes too readily, will fall victim to the charlatan. To him, if a statement sounds true it is true. The world is full of those with the proclivity or willingness to believe. We need to question more than we normally do. Peter Abelard said, "It is through doubt that one comes to investigation, and through investigation that one comes to truth."

On the other hand, the person who goes through life a complete skeptic is as sealed off from the world of reality as the person who goes through life adhering to one closed system of thought. The complete skeptic who believes in nothing is living in his own empty world. What we need, says Bertrand Russell, is intelligent skepticism. This is the essence of the scientific method.

16
Those know-it-alls

I am continually amused by sports commentator Howard Cosell and others who continually presume to have knowledge that they don't have.

When Cosell came to San Diego to broadcast the fight between Ken Norton and Muhammad Ali, Cosell called it a mismatch, he said that the fight never should have been sanctioned. He admitted that he knew nothing about Norton but he had his opinions. After seeing him in several fights with Muhammad Ali he admitted that he was a good fighter. When heavyweight champion Larry Holmes fought Norton he downgraded his abilities also. Now, he concedes, Holmes is a better fighter than he thought he was.

Cosell illustrates what many people fall victim to, they presume to have knowledge that they don't have. The unfortunate thing about a person in Cosell's position, however, is that he has the power of television, the most powerful medium known to man. He can criticize an athlete on television and make him look even worse than he looked in the contest. Everyone makes mistakes but it is more unfortunate when that mistake is in plain view of millions of people.

It has long been recognized that those who can't do anything themselves tend to knock others. You never find a great athlete like Frank Gifford knocking athletes because he knows how difficult their job is, they are the best in their profession, and everyone will make an error or a mistake.

Big people just don't knock others, they are above this immature and childish behavior.

People who assume knowledge that they don't have are guilty of what the general semanticist calls the "allness orientation," the assumption that they know it all. This is afflicted with "allness." Some people are psychologically unable to say "I don't know." And when you are unable to say "I don't know," you then presume to have knowledge that you don't have. You pass off inferences and assumptions as if they were factual and you behave that way too.

One of the most important things that you and I can do is to say "I don't know." There is so much knowledge and information in the world that no one can know everything about everything. We are tremendously limited in our acquaintance with things. If we don't know about something we should be willing to admit our own ignorance. Those who refuse to admit their ignorance get themselves and their companies into trouble.

People who refuse to say "I don't know" seldom search for the answers. Those afflicted with "allness" put a period or an exclamation mark after their statement, as if no more can be said. This "know it all" attitude is an over compensation for a feeling of intellectual inadequacy. It is a poor quality for any leader.

Those who are psychologically able to say "I don't know" usually search further for the answers. This is the scientific attitude. The motto is, "I don't know. Let's see." This leads toward further learning, testing, and searching. It is characteristic of an open mind.

The person with an open mind is what my professor at Northwestern University, Dr. Irving J. Lee, called a "viable man." He described this person in the following manner:

"Viable — capable of living or developing, as viable seeds, physically and psychologically fitted to live and grow.

"I know some viable men. They keep pushing beyond the horizons of what they already know. They refuse to be stuck in yesterday. They won't even remain rooted in today.

"They are teachable. They keep learning. They continue

to see and listen. All their horizons are temporary. They don't deny today's wisdom — rather they add dimensions to it," he said.

"They have strong faiths, belief, aspirations, but they know the difference between belief and bigotry — between knowledge and dogmatism. They are acutely aware of the limits of what they know.

"They are more likely to wonder and inquire than to dismiss and deny. They know a great deal, but they also know that they do not know it all.

"I also know some stunted, deadened men. Their outlooks have been blighted — their interests diminished — their enthusiasm restricted — their sensitivity limited.

"They are the old fogies, though they may be young in years. They strive only to stay where they are. They see only the dimensions of what has already been explored. They search with their eyes only for what is old and familiar. They have frozen their views in molds.

"They have narrowed the waves lengths. They are imprisoned in the little community — the little dusty dungeons of their own minds. They are the conflict carriers."

17
Mental rigidity detailed

Two of the most important words in psychology and the human condition are rigidity and spontaneity. You can see it in a person's attitude, you can hear it in his talk, and you can observe it in his behavior. Some people are so rigid in their responses toward others that you can almost predict their behavior. Others are so spontaneous that you can never be sure what their next move will be. They are the movers of the world.

Those who are rigid in their behavior are "other-directed." They are conditioned like Pavlov's dogs. They have stereotyped reactions toward such high-order abstractions as "Blacks," "Whites," "Mexicans," "Republicans," "Democrats," and any others who happen to fall under an abstract label.

Those who are spontaneous are "inner-directed." Their thinking and their behavior is not controlled by the outside world as much as it is by themselves. They do their own specific thinking, they do not think in terms of vague generalities. They are able to change their ways of behaving because they realize that the world of reality changes and their behavior must reflect this characteristic of the structure of the world of reality.

We must all analyze ourselves. Do we have rigid, stereotyped, closed reactions toward people, situations and things? Or are we spontaneous, open and willing to change according to the changing world? Can you open up to something new or do you rigidly hang on to your accustomed behavior?

I recently had a visit from a distant cousin I had never met. He felt that his closest family was distant, bitter, never loving or caring about others in the family, while our side of the family was just the opposite. I called up his uncle, whom I knew as a youth, and he, too, did not know why his family was so distant, almost hateful, and showing no love or affection.

The uncle sounded as if he had never thought about this lack of warmth and feeling, this almost hate for each other. And he grudgingly said, "Maybe we should get together."

I feel sorry for people like this, who hold on to their hates and negative emotions for countless years, even forgetting what started the hate in the first place.

Rigid people build their own dungeons of despair. The rigid never grow. They tend to do things the same way they've always done them. They never live up to their fullest potential.

The only thing that you can truly control is your own mind. You can change your world by changing your mind. Instead of having the same old stereotyped ways of thinking and responding, try consciously, at first, to do things differently. Try responding to people, situations and things differently than you have in the past and you will see that a whole new world will open up to you.

Open-minded and spontaneous people are too happy with life to be bogged down with negative emotions. Especially the negative emotions of others. They are too busy and strong-minded to allow these negative emotions to engulf them. They are striving toward success, whatever their definition of success is, and they are not afraid to fail.

In fact, failure does not exist. They realize that failure is simply someone else's opinion of how a certain act should have been done. They pay no attention to this opinion that they have failed for they know that success is theirs as long as they keep trying.

Success is not a destination, it is a journey. There may be many road blocks and side roads that one may have to travel but success is in the traveling, not in achieving the goal.

In fact, too often this leads toward quitting. Having achieved a goal, too many people stop; they stop achieving, they stop learning, they stop living.

Try to pinpoint the areas where you are rigid and close-minded. See if you can find the causes for such unscientific rigidity and you will then realize that they belong where they began, back in the ashcan of yesterday's habits.

Rigidity is a form of psychological paralysis. The wonderful Jerry Lewis telethon has shown us many examples of the unfortunate muscular paralysis. Equally unfortunate is its psychological counterpart. But it is much more pernicious and dangerous because it is more difficult to see with the naked eye. The eye can only see outward.

18

Keep an open mind and heart

We last wrote about the "allness orientation," the assumption that we know it all, the refusal to listen, to learn, to change or keep up to date. What is the opposite of this closed mind? General semanticists call this the "non-allness orientation." The non-allness orientation is the realization that we do not know it all. This is the kind of orientation where an individual realizes the limitations of knowledge in his thinking, speaking and behaving.

The allness-oriented person tends to put a period or an exclamation point after his sentences as if to say, "This is it." The non-allness-oriented person realizes that no matter what he says, he has not exhausted all of the details of whatever he is talking about. In other words, to the non-allness-oriented person, there is always an et cetera. In fact, this is one of the devices to eliminate or lessen allness.

There is a great difference between the person who has strong beliefs about something and yet "remembers the etc.," and the person who has equally strong beliefs but "forgets the etc."

The first one is teachable. He will hear people out, he will keep an open mind, he listens to other points of view. The person who forgets the etc. closes his mind to new or novel ideas; he becomes rigid and inflexible to those people, situations or things that run contrary to his "allness opinion."

People who are willing to admit they don't know, usually acquire the incentive to do — to research and find the answers. They are the doers. On the other hand, people who always make believe they know never really try to find out what they don't know. To admit that you don't know is the beginning of wisdom, providing you then do something about it.

What are some conclusions that we might arrive at in considering the "allness" and "non-allness" orientation?

1. Wisdom begins at home. It is easy to see the allness orientation in others, but wisdom begins when you can see it in yourself. Some people cannot see it in themselves — this is a sure sign of allness.

2. We must be sure that in our talking and acting we don't start the circle of allness. The allness orientation is a learned or conditioned pattern of behavior. If we have a semantic environment of dogmatism, be it in a family, company, military group, classroom, etc., we should not be surprised if it infects all or most members of the group. However, if we have learned to be dogmatic and a "know it all," we can also unlearn it.

3. We can do a good deal of dissolving allness in others by assuming a non-allness orientation ourselves. Quietly, over a period of time, we can teach others the principles of non-allness. We don't want to fall victim to the allness orientation ourselves in trying to change the allness in others.

4. There is no necessary relationship between a person's education, intelligence and his allness. This conclusion is a sad commentary on our educational system because my experience and that of many others has been that some Ph.D.'s or M.D.'s have been extremely closed-minded about those things that fall outside of their intellectual competency. Many educated as well as uneducated people have been extremely closed-minded about those things that they know nothing about. Rather than saying, "I don't know," they say, "I don't believe," and this is the attitude of the skeptic rather than the scientist. I have had executives verify this conclusion relative to scientists in their com-

panies with a further question, "Isn't it interesting that the very men who are instrumental in changing the lives of others, are so resistant to change when it affects them?"

5. We must realize ourselves, and teach others to realize, that this allness shows itself in "all" degrees, in "all" variations, in "all" circumstances and in very subtle ways. The allness orientation is extremely subtle, manifesting itself in the refusal to listen, to learn, to change or keep up to date, to ask questions, to look or look again, to delegate responsibility — in countless ways do we see the subtle allness orientation.

Keep an open mind and an open heart in everything that you do. You will be easier to live with for others, but more importantly, you will be easier to live with for yourself!

THE IMPORTANCE
OF ATTITUDE IN
PERSONAL RELATIONS

19
Attitude points the way

The greatest difference between man and any other form of life is the human mind. It is the most powerful instrument known to science. But it can be used for either good or bad results.

With a positive mental attitude the mind can achieve amazing results. With a negative mental attitude it can go down to the depths of despair. And the most important point is that we have the power to choose which it shall be.

In my success seminars I often refer to Thomas Alva Edison as the man whose mind had the highest cash value in history. He holds the record for the most U.S. patents by an individual — 1,093. The applications and extensions of his inventions are geometric and unending, just like the human mind.

Using a filament of carbonized cotton thread in an evacuated glass bulb, he created the first practical incandescent lamp. The modern electric age had begun. By 1890, it was possible to own the following electrical appliances: the fan, cigar lighter, iron, hot plate, coffee pot, sewing machine, stew pan and soldering iron.

By 1910, the following electric-powered items were readily available: the heating pad, chafing dish, immersion heater, curling iron, frying pan, toaster, corn popper, heater, portable drill, waffle iron and chocolate warmer. By 1920, the electric stove was in many homes around America as well as the washing machine, the vacuum cleaner, the dishwasher and the hair dryer.

Further applications of electricity followed. Motors in factories and streetcars were improved and made more efficient and powerful. Edison himself had built an experimental electric railroad. In less than 15 years, more than 20,000 miles of electric streetcar railway were built and horse-drawn cars became a thing of the past.

Edison had his critics and skeptics, the "experts" who said that it couldn't be done. Theoretical scientists at the same time said that "subdivision of light" was impossible and contrary to the laws of conservation of energy. The gas lobby and envious scientists pronounced Edison an uneducated fraud and declared the subdivision of light a hoax.

When his university-trained colleagues said it was impossible to make a generator that was more than 50 percent efficient, Edison worked diligently to prove them wrong — and he did.

The history of science and the history of man is full of so-called experts who say that "it can't be done." Not realizing that, although "it can't be done," many geniuses have gone ahead and done it.

Every age is full of people with a closed mind and a negative mental attitude. Intelligent skepticism, says Bertrand Russell, is important in scientific inquiry. Peter Abelard wrote about the importance of doubt, of not believing everything that you hear or read. But coupled with doubt and intelligent skepticism is an open mind, the ability to say, "I don't know. Let's see." This is the philosophy of the scientist.

Too many people criticize or reject new ideas without the requisite knowledge. They presume to have knowledge that they don't have. They refuse to say, "I don't know." And so their opinions are passed off as though they were factual statements.

It is extremely difficult for some of us to admit our own ignorance and yet this is one of the most important things that we can do. For when we admit our own ignorance we then seek to find the answer. There is nothing so exasperating as the ignorant person who thinks he knows it all.

All of us are ignorant in every area, so great and detailed

are the facts of any situation. Not to admit your ignorance and not do anything about it is one thing. But to admit your ignorance and then do something about it is something else again. This is the attitude of the scientist, the scholar, the intelligent person.

Ignorance is merely lack of knowledge. Stupidity, however, comes in many forms. It shows itself when we have opinions about people, situations, or things about which we have no factual data. Stupidity is evident when we refuse to change our ways of thinking in spite of the facts because we have already made up our minds. Fifty years ago we used to call it "stubbornness." Today we know it as stupidity.

Herbert Spencer has said, "There is a principle which is a bar against all information; which is proof against all argument; and which cannot fail to keep a man in everlasting ignorance. This principle is contempt prior to examination."

20
Attitudes pose problems

One of the biggest problems that people have is with their attitudes, the unconscious determinants of behavior. The subject of attitudes has been neglected among academic and industrial training programs.

It has not been sufficiently realized that attitudes, attitude training and application provide the platform for morale, enthusiasm and achievement. It is even highly possible that all inventive breakthroughs by creative persons have come as a result of an attitude change on their part. Change the attitude and you change the result.

What does attitude-control do for a spaceship? It provides a level platform from which the astronauts can operate and navigate the vehicle. The vehicle maintains its balance with a given point of reference such as the horizon, a star, etc. This is exactly what an attitude attempts to do for its holder. Attitudes provide platforms from which we all operate. They control our own personal balance or imbalance.

What is an attitude? An attitude is an observable behavior which is repetitive under similar circumstances. Sometimes an attitude is called a state of mind, a fixed or rigid response to similar circumstances.

Perhaps we can better understand attitudes if we listed a few of the more general positive and negative attitudes that we see operating in the world today. We will also be able to see how these attitudes lead toward certain kinds of behavior.

A positive attitude is often seen with the open-minded person, whereas the negative attitude is characteristic of the close-minded. The open-minded person has a positive attitude about everything while the closed-minded person shuts his mind off to new experiences.

The positive attitude judges people, situations and things here and now, whereas the negative attitude prejudges people, situations and things. This is, of course, what we mean by prejudice. People with negative attitudes waste hard-earned money going to a play or the theater to have a miserable time. And all they had to change was their attitude in order to have a pleasurable experience. Unconscious attitudes control us more than we realize.

The person with a positive attitude is usually enthusiastic while the one with a negative attitude is morose and sullen. Enthusiasm is one of the most important words for success and happiness, and it can be learned just as easily as its opposite.

Positive people are usually healthy while negative attitudes create sickness. Holistic medicine has shown the important relationship between the mind and physical well-being. More sickness and physical ills are created by a negative attitude than people realize. This is why medical doctors should know more about psychiatry.

A person with a positive attitude is awake and aware while the person with a negative attitude is asleep. As someone once said, "A few people make things happen, some people see things happen, while most people don't know that anything happened at all!" This is why the teachers of success motivation want to awaken that sleeping giant within you. Everyone would have a much greater potential if he or she would just awaken and realize the vast inner resources nature has given us.

A person with a positive attitude is usually successful while the negative attitude leads to failure. "Attitude" is what Earl Nightingale calls "the magic word." It is the most important element of success or failure.

A positive attitude leads toward safety while the negative attitude leads toward accidents. It is no secret to psychiatrists that accident-prone people have negative attitudes, psychological problems, or an unconscious wish to hurt themselves or others. Attitudes are the result of unconscious assumptions and a person's behavior results from both.

Since most attitudes are developed for security reasons at an early age, most of us are not conscious of the large percentage of our attitudes. And yet it is the same attitudes that determine what we are and what we become.

Our attitudes toward the world are identical with the ones we have toward ourselves. If we hate ourselves, we hate the world. To the degree we lie to ourselves, to that same degree we lie to everyone else. There is one important difference, however. We rarely blame ourselves for failure. Rather, we place the responsibility elsewhere.

Remember that an attitude is like a magnet; it attracts what it feels about itself and what it accepts from others. Unfortunately, there is no legal protection against those who, either by design or ignorance, poison the minds of others by negative attitudes.

21
Getting along with others

There have been many surveys taken in business and industry relative to the kind of person that an employer will hire and the important qualification usually comes down to "the ability to get along with others." This has been called the art of human relations, and human relations courses have had their share of critics as well as champions.

Those who champion the cause of human relations realize that work is always done by and with the help of people. Business and industry have become more people oriented, and for good reason. People are not the same as they were 40 years ago. New motivational techniques must be used, and successful leaders must apply the art of human relations.

One key to success in human relations is empathy. Empathy is the ability to put yourself in another person's shoes; to see things from his or her point of view, to feel as they do. Most of us are so egocentric that we only think about things from our own point of view. And this is bound to cause problems.

Some experts have gone so far as to say, "Until you make an effort to feel as another person does, you will not understand human relations." It is important to recognize that empathy is not sympathy. It is entirely possible to sympathize with a person without ever feeling empathy for him or her.

There are many areas in one's personal and professional life where empathy is important. And the ability to place yourself in the other person's position is a quality that can be developed. It can lead to success in many areas of human relations.

For example, salespeople can succeed much more quickly by developing the habit of placing themselves in the position of buyers they are trying to sell to. How many businesses can you think of that never once seem to put themselves in the position of the customer?

Empathy is extremely important in the art of communication. In fact, Dr. Carl Rogers' non-directive counseling is centered on this important art. The ability to listen with empathy is extremely important whether you are listening as an executive, a teacher, a parent, or just in everyday ordinary conversation. We so often say, "I know what you mean," but seldom do we really know what the other person means because we don't take his needs, wants and desires into consideration.

Another way of improving our human relations is understanding how to handle criticism. Most of us cannot handle criticism because our ego is too involved. Many people can't stand criticism of any kind. The reason is that many of us are so unsure of ourselves that we take criticism personally and it shakes our ego. We take the criticism as an attack on ourselves and never listen to see whether we can learn or profit from it.

And so we reject what might be the most important communication for our personal change and improvement. Some people are constantly criticizing others; they are the perpetual complainers in life, and they usually tell more about themselves than about whom they are talking. This is negative criticism.

But there is positive criticism, the kind of criticism that will point out what you have been doing wrong, and showing you how to do it correctly. There is criticism whose motive is to help, not hinder, and this is the kind of criticism that we must learn to take.

Change and growth go together. When we can accept criticism and change we then begin to grow. When we cannot do this, then we guarantee that we will never grow.

How can anyone change himself for the better when he closes his mind to all positive suggestions?

How can we learn to get along with others? Getting along with people is easy for some of us, while for others it is a difficult if not impossible task. Why do some people find it so difficult to get along with others, to have good human relations? One reason is because they think of themselves too much. They are too preoccupied with their own selves. There are many requirements for achieving interpersonal relationships, but there is a simple, three-step formula which you can apply.

1. Be yourself. Try to act as you really are, don't try to be someone else. The phony is easily detected. This false front breaks down in the long run, and the result will be that others will not trust the person who acts in this manner.

2. Be happy with what you are. It is difficult for others to like us if we don't like ourselves. An individual who doesn't like himself will feel inadequate, second rate, or a failure in life. And, though others may feel sorry for him, they will dislike him because of this negative attitude.

3. Our actions must be acceptable to others. We should act within socially acceptable limits. The criminal mentality is not acceptable to others because it violates the rights of others. Remember that we can't get along with others unless they also accept what we do or what we are. This is the heart of human relations.

22
Small talk is important

In our classes in general semantics and effective communication, we teach people how to think, communicate, and behave intelligently. By intelligently we mean that our evaluations must fit the facts. This is what we call "serious" talk.

There is another kind of communication, however, which is equally important, but in which we are not concerned with proper evaluation. This is in the area of "small talk."

Many people play down the importance of small talk. Many are deficient in their ability to engage in small talk. In teaching executives for many years I have found that engineers have been, as a group (realizing the dangers of generalizing), deficient in the ability to engage in small talk.

It is true that in some business or industrial organizations there can be too much small talk. Sometimes too much time is wasted with too much of it. But small talk is an important part of every organization. People need to feel free to communicate with others for psychological purposes.

This brings us to the important purpose of small talk. It is psychological in nature. Man is a gregarious being and he needs to tap the psyche of others. He needs the feeling of belonging, of being loved or liked, of sharing and living with others. And he does this through small talk.

What is the worst punishment, short of physical torture, that you can give to a prisoner? It is solitary confinement.

Man needs to communicate with others. And those who do not understand the importance of small talk will always accuse others of saying silly or unimportant things when they ask, "Nice weather, isn't it.?"

If you were driving along the road in your automobile and got a flat tire on a broiling hot day, and someone came by and asked you, "Got a flat?" what would your answer be? Probably not too pleasant. Dr. Karl Menninger mentions such a case in *Love Against Hate*. The motorist pulls off the road and makes preparation to change the tire. At that moment a farmer strolls up and asks the obvious question, "Gotta flat?"

According to Dr. Menninger, the psychological meaning of such a question is an awkward but conventionalized way of saying something like this to the motorist:

"Hello — I see you're in trouble. I'm a stranger to you but I might be your friend now that I have a chance to be, if I had any assurance that my friendship would be welcomed. Are you approachable? Are you a decent fellow? Would you appreciate it if I helped? I'd like to do so but I don't want to be rebuffed. This is what my voice sounds like. What does your voice sound like?"

This could be done in a more direct way, such as saying, "I'd be glad to help you, stranger." But as Dr. Menninger points out, people often are too timid and mutually distrustful to be so direct. They want to hear the other person's voice to get reassurance that others are like themselves. Not as much content goes into the apparently trite question as "Hot enough for you?" or "How do you feel?" but much the same psychological mechanism is at work. It is a means of establishing good will, sociability and communion with others. Maturity or growing up implies learning to understand what people really mean when they say obvious things.

The general semanticist considers two different kinds of silence. Silence we might define as a "good" kind of silence, is where we stop talking and think or act. This kind of silence in today's world is a rare and precious commodity to the scholar or thinker. Silence can also be a "bad" kind of silence. For example, at a social party, silence can convey the feeling of hostility, dislike or uneasiness.

If you think about it, those whom we define as "popular," "well-liked," or who possess poise have the ability to engage in small talk. They are easy to be around. There are others who find small talk difficult, silly, or not worthwhile. These are very often the problem-people in business and industry.

The ability to get along with others is one of the most important qualities that people look for in hiring. And if you think about it this comes down to the ability to communicate or engage freely and comfortably in small talk.

Ask yourself, "Am I deficient in small talk?" If you are, do something about it. Start now to engage in more small talk and you will see that a whole new world will open up to you. H.G. Wells has said, "Words are sometimes only spoken to break the tension of silence." Perhaps Thomas Mann summed it up best when he said, "Effective speech is civilization itself. Silence isolates, words draw us together."

23

Beware of snap judgments

I am often amused by friends of mine. People continually ask them what I am really like.

They are surprised when my friends tell them that I am just average, like anyone else, don't drive a Rolls-Royce, take them to Wendy's Hamburgers rather than Mister A's and am "low key" at the office or recording studio. They say that I am completely different than people think I am.

This brings up several important points. The picture inside our heads is never the same as the world of reality. The picture that we have of another person is never his or her true self. And yet most of us make snap judgments about people and act as if "that's how they really are" — always.

We do not realize that the picture inside our heads is merely an abstraction and this is why each of us has a different picture of everyone and everything.

And when we meet that person we are surprised because he or she does not fit the false-to-fact picture inside our heads that we shouldn't have had in the first place. Rather than trying to make the world of reality fit the picture that we have inside our heads, we should try to make the picture inside our heads fit the world of reality.

One of the things that general semantics teaches us is to try to make our thinking and our behavior fit the structure of the world of reality, to fit the facts. Most of us reverse the process. If we don't know anything about a person we should be able to say, "I don't know." But we don't do that.

We presume to have knowledge about a person through an abstract label, one of many labels that we can apply to any person, and we act as if the label were the person, or as if our definition of the person is the person.

By saying "I don't know" we withhold judgment and allow the facts to be paramount. By observing facts first we can then use words to describe those facts and our language will more closely approximate the world of reality.

How can we learn to be more scientific in our everyday thinking and behavior?

1. Remember that the word is not the thing. The words that we use in describing or defining things are not the same as the nonverbal objects.

2. Remember that the picture inside our heads is not the same as the world of reality. They are on different levels of abstraction. But in order to maintain sanity and get along well in this world the picture inside our heads should approximate or adequately represent the world of reality. A map that is false-to-fact can only lead to chaos.

3. Remember that life is a series of assumptions and too many of us have false assumptions about people, situations, and things. And too often we confuse our assumptions with facts and refuse to change them.

4. Try to pause, delay, and analyze more than you normally do. Too many people have automatic, trigger-like reactions. They make snap judgments. By pausing and delaying your responses you can observe the world of reality more adequately and then make your language or assumptions fit the facts.

5. Be magnanimous in your observations and verbalizations about others. Small people continually criticize others or carp about things. Big people don't need to build themselves up by tearing other people down. They realize that their own verbalizations tell more about themselves than the people about whom they are talking.

24

The art of human relations

Professor Wallace Brett Donham of Harvard, and associates from other universities, present 10 simple rules for keeping out, or getting out, of trouble.

1. Learn all about a problem before trying to solve it. Listen a lot. Talk a little. Although we cannot know "all" about anything, too many of us presume to have more knowledge than we really have. In solving problems we must try to get as much factual data as we possibly can. And after getting as much evidence as we can, go ahead and make the decision. Don't procrastinate. No decision at all is often worse than a bad one. Especially if this gets to be a habitual pattern.

2. See the total situation. Don't act on just a part of it. Here, too, we must try to see the situation as a whole. It is so easy for us to abstract or select a small part for our own convenience and leave out the most essential part of the situation. This means that we must be as objective as we possibly can and realize the subjectivity of human perception.

3. Don't be deceived by logic. Most problems are full of emotion. You cannot leave out the human being from situations, and people are full of emotions. Most problems, even those that seemingly are devoid of emotionality, are full of emotional feeling. Recognize your own emotions and try to be more objective while asking other people to do the same.

4. Watch for the ambiguity of language and the many meanings of words. Look behind words to get their full impact. Realize that other people have had different experiences than you and, therefore, give different meanings to words. Meanings are not in words — they are in people. And you must ask others what they mean before criticizing or disagreeing with them.

5. No moral judgments, please. Until you have diagnosed a problem, don't leap to conclusions about what's right and what's wrong. Too many of us jump to conclusions too quickly. We are too ready with our own moral judgments without trying to understand the situation from other points of view. To the degree that we moralize, to that degree do we fail to analyze.

6. Imagine yourself in the other person's shoes. See how the problem looks from where he or she sits. One of the most important words in management, in teaching, in being a parent, in life generally, is the word "empathy." We must learn to listen with empathy. We must keep an open mind and an open heart in dealing with people, in trying to understand them and their problems from their point of view. Too many of us are self-centered and egotistical, unable to feel the emotions of others as they feel them. We could if we tried, and this is empathy.

7. When a problem gets you down, get away from it. Put it in the back of your mind for a week. When you approach it again, the solution may be obvious. Sometimes we are so close to the forest we fail to see the trees. Get away for a while and rejuvenate your energies. Stop thinking hard for a solution, relax your conscious mind, and let your subconscious mind take over. You will be surprised at how a solution will "pop out." This is inspiration and creative imagination at work.

8. Ask yourself, "What are the forces acting upon the other fellow? Why does he behave as he does?" Few of us really try to analyze why other people behave as they do. We are quick to criticize, to moralize, to pass judgment, but slow to understand or empathize. I have a statement that I tell my students, "Never criticize others until you know

why they are doing what they are doing from their point of view!" Too many of us think that *our* world of reality, *our* perception of the world, is the only one, the right one. Such an attitude can only lead to conflict. We must realize that other people's point of view, while different from our own, can be equally valid and correct. Ours or theirs is not necessarily better but just different. And difference is a characteristic of various human perceptions.

9. Diagnosis must come before action. Use the doctor's approach. Don't prescribe until you're sure what is wrong. Be as scientific outside of the laboratory as the scientist is inside the laboratory. This means pausing and delaying your reactions, keeping an open mind, not projecting your feelings into the situation. And using your eyes and ears more than your mouth. No one has ever learned anything while talking.

10. Easy does it. Quick solutions are often the quick route to trouble. Take your time. Count to 10 before talking or reacting.

LIVING IN A
NON-VERBAL WORLD

25
Science deals in probables

The headlines boldly proclaimed, "Mystics Read Signs, Come Up With Chargers." It goes on to say, "Setting a mystical morning line, a psychic, a spiritualist and an astrologer peered into the great beyond yesterday and reported sighting an AFC championship for the San Diego Chargers." One spiritualist who reads bumps and palms said that Dan Fouts' astrological chart — he is a Gemini — shows that "nothing is going to stop him and the Chargers from going to the Super Bowl." Except, maybe, the Oakland Raiders. I say "maybe" because any prediction about the future is tentative, except natural laws which have a high degree of predictability.

An astrologer said, "The other guy (Raiders quarterback Jim Plunkett) is a Sagittarius, and Sunday will not be the right time for him to be playing against a team led by a Gemini. The Chargers will win by a big score." But another astrologer, presumably using similar "facts" had an opposite prediction. She specializes in astrological forecasts of horse races and predicted that the Chargers will win a narrow victory, with the final scoring play probably deciding the game. She said, "The planets will lean to Oakland in the early portion of the game but will tilt toward San Diego in the home stretch to ensure victory for the Chargers."

To them, if you want to know who is going to win the game and why, you look to the heavens rather than to what happens on Earth. The completed passes, the missed tackles and extra points or field goals, the long runs, are not as important as the position of the stars, or whatever their guesses are based upon. It was interesting to note that an Oakland astrologer said, "I don't know nothing about football but Oakland is going to win." It appears that the heavenly bodies are different in Oakland.

Scientists, for years, have been concerned about the unscientific fluff that has been perpetrated upon the unintelligent public. And now it appears that newspapers, radio and television are helping to expand an antiscientific attitude.

One radio station is featuring a weekly interview with an astrologer who gives all kinds of advice to all kinds of people on the basis of when they were born. She gives the usual generalizations that common sense would dictate and what people would like to hear. But she never says, "I don't know," which is the trademark of the scientist. The possessor of an unscientific mind presumes to have knowledge which he or she doesn't have and will give "factually sounding" answers on all problems.

This is another of the problems dealing with the unscientific method. People think that they are dealing with "facts" when they are only dealing with words, figures, symbols or other aspects of the verbal world.

Science deals with the non-verbal world which can be empirically tested by other scientists. It is based upon factual evidence, not a string of symbols, words or figures which appear to be factual.

This was one of the problems in formal logic for many years. It was assumed that Aristotelian deductive logic had something to do with the world of reality. Later on, Roger and Francis Bacon and other logicians showed that deductive logic is only a relationship between the first premise, second premise and the conclusion. Deductive logic deals with validity, how valid one premise is arising from the other, and whether or not the conclusion follows. Deductive or formal logic has nothing to do with the world of reality; it is a linguistic, formal, tautological relationship based upon verbal definition or agreement.

Inductive logic deals with the world of reality, based upon facts, and its conclusions are, therefore, probable rather than certain. Heisenberg's Uncertainty Principle has shown us that the moment we talk about the world of reality we are in the area of probability, not certainty.

Having these "formulas" based upon words, charts, figures, symbols or any other part of the verbal world does not make it factual. It is still a part of the **ARBITRARY** verbal world. But most people are ignorant of this verbal-non-verbal confusion and they accept verbal analyses for factual evidence.

It is worse yet when these unscientific people give business or personal advice, because it can keep you from going to a person whose advice is based upon factual evidence. If you want advice in your business affairs you go to your CPA, banker or business consultant who has experience in these matters. If you want advice on physical or mental health problems you go to a medical doctor, a clinical psychologist or a psychiatrist.

26
Be aware of charlatans

In my last column I wrote about the necessity of orienting our lives around facts rather than words.

This is an important distinction to the general semanticist. General semantics points out two different orientations in life. The intensional orientation is characterized by reacting to people, situations and things in terms of words and verbal associations. Most of us are verbally oriented because our educational institutions very often do not make the important distinction between words and things.

In the intensional orientation, we confuse verbal "proofs" with factual proof. If something sounds true, we think that it is true, when in reality we have no way of checking whether or not it is true.

This overemphasis on words, giving them false "factual existence," has aided the charlatan for centuries. It is well-known how poor, ignorant people are "taken" when they believe the empty words of verbal manipulators. But it is not limited to the uneducated. A university professor testified in court that spirit voices called up by a woman preacher led him to invest $16,000 in a dry oil well, a non-existent Mexican fortune and a company which later went bankrupt.

We continually read similar cases in newspapers where people act as if words necessarily indicate factual existence. To them, the word IS the thing. If you have a word you must have the something it stands for. But as these intensionally or verbally oriented people have sadly discovered, whether buying non-existent property or receiving a worthless check, the piece of paper is not what it is supposed to represent.

When the astrologers predicted that the San Diego Chargers would defeat the Oakland Raiders after reading their astrological charts, we only had to wait a few days after the game to determine the truth of their assertion. And we saw that their assertion had no basis in fact. The whole history of fortune-telling, astrology and other forms of predictions into the future are examples of an intensional orientation. They are obviously not based upon facts, because the fact has not occurred yet. They are based upon inferences, guesses, assumptions and beliefs, passed off as if they were factual.

The extensional orientation is the opposite of the intensional one. The extensional orientation is based upon facts and testing, and is characterized by the scientific method. You base your judgment not on what people say, but what they do. You don't confuse verbal statements with factual observations. You don't accept other people's verbal assertions as if they are factual. You say, "I don't know." And you wait for more evidence.

If you adopt the extensional orientation of the scientist in place of the intensional orientation of the verbally oriented, you will find many rewards. You will not be "taken in" by the con man or the verbal manipulators who try to skew the world of reality in their favor by the use of words.

Dr. S.I. Hayakawa once said, "The rewards in this world go to those who talk fast, not sense." And this, unfortunately, is too often true. We must have a built-in doubt — an intelligent skepticism — to keep us from being victimized by the verbal manipulators.

When the proverbial man from Missouri said, "Show me," he was behaving extensionally. The whole history of science has been the extensional orientation of factual proof, testing, retesting and allowing others to test a verbal assertion or hypothesis.

This extensional orientation is especially important in business and in life. Many businesses have gone broke because they did not do their homework. They assumed that there was a need for their product or service when there wasn't. They sadly learned that assumptions are not the same as facts.

You and I must learn to be more questioning and demand more factual evidence in everything we do. Do not accept the assumptions of others, or yourself, as if they were factual. Check them. Test them. Do not confuse verbal statements with factual data. Be more scientific in your everyday life. You will be amazed at how much more successful you will be in business as well as in life generally.

27
Words can mislead you

The famous biologist Louis Agassiz said, "If you study nature in books, when you go out of doors you cannot find her." Most of our education is verbal rather than factual. And it is no wonder that we have generations of people who confuse words with facts, the verbal world of reality with the factual.

There is no discipline that I know of, other than general semantics, that accentuates the important point that "the word is not the thing." We are living in two different worlds of reality, the verbal world and the non-verbal world, and too many of our problems are caused by the confusion of words and things.

Because our educational institutions do not emphasize this important distinction, we have students and adults who react as if all "actors" or "actresses," "psychiatrists," "teachers," "hypnotists" — all of anything — are the same. This is the easiest way to go through life. This is the kind of thinking we do when we don't do any thinking. It takes a certain amount of intelligence and gray matter to see that people are not only similar but that there are important differences among them.

People who see only the label also see only the similarities while the differences are the most important. We stereotype people when we react to them only in terms of the label. We do the greatest injustice to them as well as to ourselves.

Although many serious students of hypnosis have been

attempting to study and elevate the science and art, there have been a disproportionate number who have misused it. Hypnosis has attracted too many con artists and charlatans, a disproportionate number of psychopaths and sociopaths. These are individuals who are liars, cheats and swindlers, those who have no conscience or ethics. And even today we see hypnosis being used by some in a very unethical way, controlling the behavior of others and not allowing them to think for themselves.

The most important thing that education does is to teach students how to think, and some agencies are operating today depriving some individuals of this most important human attribute. Through hypnosis and mind control, they are reducing them into automatons or robots, and most people have no idea of what is going on.

Belief is important in many areas of life, but when you believe in others more than you believe in your own ability to think, then you are giving over to others the most important characteristic of man, the ability to think.

We must teach our students and adults how to think intelligently, and this means being able to differentiate between words and generalizations and the factual world of reality. This is a discipline that can and must be taught if we are going to have a generation of adults who are able to cope with the barrage of verbiage and suggestions that are being given us at an accelerated rate through our media.

What I am saying is nothing new. Some of our greatest scholars have said the same thing for many years. Sigmund Freud said, "I have held fast to the habit of always studying things before looking for information about them in books."

Confucius many years ago said, "Wishing to think sincerely, they first extended their knowledge. This they did by investigation of things. By investigation of things their knowledge became extensive. Their knowledge became extensive, their thought became sincere."

And in the Analects he said, "At first, my way with men was to hear their words and give them credit for their conduct. Now my way is to hear their words and look at their conduct."

The famous mathematician Herman Weyl perhaps said it best: "Indeed, the first difficulty the man in the street encounters when he is taught to think mathematically is that he must learn to look things much more squarely in the face; his belief in words must be shattered, he must learn to think concretely."

Yes, we must learn to think concretely. We must take more time to pause, delay and analyze the world of reality. We must know the difference between words and facts and behave accordingly. We must learn how to trust our own thinking while constantly striving to improve and get more factual data. We can and must be scientific in everything that we do. And the beginning of the scientific method is reliance on non-verbal facts rather than the verbalization of others.

28
We don't use our minds

Man has the amazing faculty of acting intelligently or stupidly. We all catch ourselves behaving "stupidly" when we fail to think intelligently, and we laugh at our unawareness afterward.

Being aware, or "awareness," is one definition of intelligence. Not being aware, or being in a "sleepwalking state," is a characteristic of lack of intelligence. And too many of us are in a sleepwalking state — we don't use our conscious mind to think and behave intelligently.

Man's ability to act unintelligently in a universe of intelligence is amazing. One example of lack of intelligence is the making of wrong decisions. One of the most important things that you and I do in everyday life is make decisions. As a result of our wrong decisions, we limit ourselves with financial problems, family quarrels, business problems and poor human relations.

Modern science proves the universe to be an arena of intelligence known as order premised upon law. Law and order are as inherent in man as they are in the universal scheme of things. And when we violate these logical laws of cause and effect, we get ourselves into trouble.

If you analyze human thinking and human problems, you will see that troubles result when an unintelligent factor is introduced into a field of intelligent activity. People have communication and human-relations problems when they jump to conclusions, when they have false assumptions about the "real" nature of things. When we project our own false notions about a situation into the situation, we display unintelligence that leads to further difficulties.

All of the negatives known to man are examples of unintelligent thinking. A negative mental attitude is one of the most dangerous examples of unintelligent thinking. It results in presuming to have knowledge about other people that we don't really have. It results in a low estimation of ourselves, thereby insuring failure. It is unintelligent because it does not allow us to live up to our fullest potential and achieve a happy, productive life.

The negative emotions of worry, hate, envy, jealousy and greed are examples of unintelligent thinking. Worry is an unintelligent factor, as usually the things we worry about never materialize. In other words we often worry about a fiction, something that doesn't exist in the world of reality, but only in our mind. This is an example of living in fantasy, not in the world of reality.

Hate, and its counterpart, self-hate, are examples of unintelligent thinking. We hate or dislike ourselves because we don't compare favorably with others, and we hate or dislike others for the same reason.

Jealousy and envy are examples of unintelligent thinking, resulting from the false notion of lack in ourselves and the world we live in. Lack is not a characteristic of ourselves and the world of reality. Abundance is, and the quicker we realize this, the quicker we will achieve what we would like to achieve and eliminate envy and jealousy. Intelligent thinking is the realization of abundance in all of life and finding the methods of achieving it.

In contrast to animals, the intelligent use of the mind is characteristic of human existence. Intelligence, cause and effect, law and order should shape our lives. Worry, fear, argument and frustration are not your normal heritage. They are abnormal, unhealthy uses of mind and emotion that you have wrongly assumed to be necessary to your everyday living.

You might argue that these negatives are normal because everyone has them. But all the sickness in the world cannot disprove health as normal. If you observe what people want in life you will see that health, joy, plenty, love and self-expression are the normal modes of living. And they can only be achieved by the intelligent use of the mind.

If you are to think intelligently, you must have a new self-awareness about yourself. The redundancy is for emphasis. You must change the self-image that you have. You cannot go beyond your own self-accepted image. As long as you underestimate yourself, you cannot succeed in life. No person IS stupid. Stupidity is only a misuse of intelligence in non-intelligent ways.

29
Controlling our expectations

We create our own happiness or misery by the expectations that we have. Many people do not realize that the mind controls the key to happiness and an important key is our expectations.

By expectation I mean "expecting to get something with certainty." When we expect to get something we are certain that it will fall our way. And so the false notion of certainty plays havoc with our life because, as Einstein and Heisenberg's "uncertainty principle" have shown, there is no such thing as certainty in the world of reality, except by definition in logic and mathematics.

This principle of uncertainty is important in everyday life. You cannot control all of the variables outside of you, but you can control the one factor that can control, to a degree, the variables outside of you. You can control your mind — and you can control your expectations.

One of the reasons why some people are frustrated and demoralized is because they don't achieve what they expected. Some people expect too much and place unrealistic expectations upon themselves and others.

You can mentally separate your expectations from your motivation, drive, goal, or ambition. Keep your motivation high but you must learn to make your expectations realistic. This means, in many cases, lowering your expectations. This will in no way affect your motivation, goal, drive, or desire if you separate the two. And you can, mentally.

The problem for most of us lies not in having expectations but in managing them, in making them work. The origin of our hopes isn't nearly as important as what we decide to do with them.

Some dreams are worth hanging on to, while others are not. Some may be reasonable for you, but ridiculous for others. Some may take us a long way toward a goal we've set up — and some may take us right over the rainbow and into the brink.

Perhaps we all deceive ourselves with fantasies and unrealistic expectations. All of us put on the rose-colored glasses from time to time, and many of us are masters of the art of self-deception.

The lines run something like this: If I were beautiful or handsome; if I had more money; if I were famous; if all the people in my office weren't such rats; if I were only born on the other side of the track. If, if, if. If all kinds of things were different, I would be happy and life would be perfect.

We play these tricks on ourselves, wait for our luck to change without doing anything about it. When things don't work our way, we groan, complain loudly about everybody and everything except ourselves, drink too much, eat too much — anything to keep from dealing with reality.

We do everything possible to prolong certain rosy dreams that are never going to come true until we learn to apply good sense and either cross them off our lists or figure out how to manage them.

We need not keep on deceiving ourselves over and over again. We can learn to manage our expectations intelligently and the key to managing your expectations and winning more of the good times is not known when you're just kidding yourself.

There may not be any absolute rules for getting exactly what you want in life, but there are some general directions and a number of do's and don'ts that could apply to all of us:

1. Don't hang on to expectations you were meant to unload 10 years ago. The world of reality changes and your expectations must change with it. Some people live in a dream world of false expectations and fantasies which

perpetuate a child-like existence. Maturity means being realistic about yourself today. If you have difficulty in differentiating between fantasy and reality it would be wise to consult a good psychologist or psychiatrist. They are experts in pointing out the false assumptions that we have about ourselves.

2. Be realistic enough to know that a fantasy that is too grand can prevent useful changes. Wildly inflated expectations can often keep you from taking the small but important steps that really do improve your life. Some people are so paralyzed by the fear of not being good enough, of not measuring up to their own or other people's expectations, that they don't do anything. Wildly inflated expectations can be a killer, but there's an even more treacherous foe to keep us from successfully managing our expectations: fear of success.

3. Don't let the fear of finally realizing your hopes keep you from making changes. It is important not to be afraid to begin, even to fail occasionally. It is also important not to cheat yourself out of what you deserve. The fear of success can be a real crippler.

4. Try to strike a balance between too many high expectations and, if you cannot separate expectations from motivation, those that are too low or self-defeating. You must also strike a balance between those that are too rigid and those that are too vague. Expectations that are very hazy — such as wanting to be happy or wanting to have a good life are too vague and ill-defined.

30
Why is man different?

I have just returned from Chicago, where I attended the funeral of my brother-in-law. And while I was on the airplane I read something of the centennial and life of Albert Einstein. These events made me think about one's contributions to society and future generations during one's lifetime. Some people's lives make hardly a dent into the future, while others' have changed the world.

This is one of the truly characteristic features of man. Alfred Korzybski, who developed general semantics, called this unique characteristic "time-binding." In his book, *Manhood of Humanity*, Korzybski said that man is not an animal. However, we can behave like animals and rationalize our animalistic ways of behaving.

Man has been defined in many different ways. Aristotle said that man is a rational animal. Some say that man is a featherless biped.

As we can see in the many examples of fights, arguments, disagreements, and killings, we have a long way to go before calling ourselves "rational." We have a potential for rationality that is much greater than animals, but there is a great amount of irrationality in our unrational human world.

What is the unique difference between man and animal and how can we evaluate man's quality of life and contribution during a lifetime? Korzybski answered this question in differentiating between plants, animals, and man.

He asked, "What is the unique characteristic of plant life?" The answer, he said, must be in terms of what they

DO, an operational definition. He concluded that plants are chemistry binding. Through the process of photosynthesis they are able to sustain life.

Now, he asked, what do animals do that plants, on the whole, do not do? His answer was that animals have the ability to move around in space. They are space binders.

Now, what about man? What is man's unique characteristic that differentiates him or her from animals? We can give many answers to this question. Animals do not have the ability to think to the degree that man does. Animals do not possess the creative imagination of man. Animals do not have the ethical, moral, or philosophical theories of man. And certainly, as far as we know, animals are not conscious of their own consciousness.

While we can give many answers to the above question, Korzybski's answer was that man, because of language, can take from the past, summarize and digest the knowledge and achievements of the past and the present, and pass on to future generations the labors of the past and the present. Korzybski called this unique characteristic in man "time binding." Man can literally "bind time."

Birds build bird nests the same way that they did hundreds of years ago. Beavers build beaver dams the same way that they did hundreds of years ago. But man, because he has language, can progress in a geometric ratio and the result of man's time binding characteristic is modern civilization.

Man is a symbolic class of life. While animals do have a form of communication, their ability differs from man, not only in degree but in kind. For example, a dog can communicate something to another dog. But as far as we know, the second dog cannot tell a third dog what the first dog told him. And the third dog cannot tell a fourth dog what each dog communicated to the other. Man, however, has unlimited orders of abstraction or symbolization. The result of this are books, libraries, universities, science, and flights to the moon. Man's potential is unlimited.

So the question is, in our own lifetime how much are we influencing the present as well as future generations? How much are we living up to our fullest potential? To what degree are we using man's unique time binding characteristic?

Each one of us can answer this in his or her own way. Dr. Jacob Bronowski filmed his great "Ascent of Man" so that future generations can learn from this brilliant scientist and teacher. His entire life, and that of other great people who lived not just for the present but for the future, benefited many generations to come. This was the genius of Einstein, changing forever man's perception of his universe — and of himself. Time binding is the unique characteristic that makes man man.